Heart to Heart

S E R I E S

Anniversary Questions

Keeping Your Marriage Healthy and Sizzling

BOBB AND CHERYL BIEHL

BROADMAN
& HOLMAN
PUBLISHERS

Nashville, Tennessee

Keeping Your Marriage Healthy and Sizzling

Published by:
Broadman & Holman Publishers
Nashville, Tennessee

Design: Steven Boyd

Printed in the United States of America

4262-73
0-8054-6273-2

Dewey Decimal Classification: 306.81
Subject Heading: MARRIAGE
Library of Congress Card Catalog Number: 95-45306

Library of Congress Cataloging-in-Publication Data
Biehl, Bobb.
    Anniversary questions: keeping your marriage healthy and
sizzling / Bobb and Cheryl Biehl
        p.   cm.—(Heart to heart series)
    ISBN 0-8054-6273-2
    1. Marriage—Miscellanea. 2. Wedding anniversaries—
Miscellanea. I. Biehl, Cheryl. II. Title. III. Series.

    HQ734.B6228   1996
    306.81—dc20

    95-45306
    CIP

00 99 98 97 96 5 4 3 2 1

Contents

Introduction

A Note from the Authors

Over our thirty-plus years of marriage, we have invested thousands of hours in counseling friends about their marriages. Most had minor differences. Most conversations were with the husband or the wife, not both together. Some were far more serious. The problems were marriage-threatening. Some, sad to say, were unsuccessful and ended in divorce.

Throughout many hours of listening, advising, pleading, coaching, and modeling, we found one key word that stands out like a 300-foot redwood tree in the middle of the west Texas flatlands. That word is: *communication!*

Married couples frequently complain:

- ✧ "We just don't have time to talk."

- ✧ "My husband is not a very good communicator. . . . I never know how he really feels."

- ✧ "We used to talk, but we don't any more."

- ✧ "How can you really communicate with someone who is always watching TV?"

⋄ "We sit at breakfast, lunch, and dinner with nothing to say to each other. . . . We have run out of things to talk about. . . . Our marriage has just gone stale."

⋄ "If we were not talking about the kids, we would be speechless."

The questions in this book can fill those awkward, dull, boring times with meaningful conversation. The best way we know of turning marriage-threatening non-communication into stimulating, growing, loving times is by asking each other bold, intimate questions—and committing to naked, open, honest, and candid answers. As you have this open communication you begin to see what is in the person's heart. You see beyond the tired face. You see beyond the aging body. You see once again the person you married and want to live with, "Till death do us part."

If this book can give you a stimulating new perspective on even a few areas in your relationship and help prevent the devastating effects of boredom, and even possibly divorce in your life five or twenty years in the future, we will feel every hour we have invested in the book's preparation was worth a thousand times the effort.

It is our hope and prayer that you will have wisdom, patience, and understanding as you work your way through these intimate, direct, profoundly simple, relationship-defining questions!

Bobb and Cheryl Biehl

PART ONE

Before You Begin

Everyone has three selves:

A public self . . .
the you that everyone in the public sees.

A private self . . .
the you that only close friends and family see
in private settings.

A personal self . . .
the you that no one has ever seen—the heart.

Chapter 1

Open the Lines of Communication

Most of the words we say are spoken in public. Some of our words are uttered in private where only old friends and family are supposed to hear them. And a few are confided in the secrecy of the marriage relationship. These words said in the protected place of marriage are words of intimacy. When there is an exchange of personal thoughts and feelings which have never before been shared with anyone, we are having an intimate heart-to-heart conversation.

Physical intimacy happens when we are allowed to have our mate's body in a manner that all others, even the closest of friends, are not. Emotional intimacy happens when we are allowed to have our mate's heart and hear things that he/she does not feel safe enough to share with any other living human being. When we are in this loved, safe, and protected place, a kind of intimate communication can happen which happens in no other place on this earth or in this life.

Certain elements in the relationship are required in order for intimacy at this level to happen:

✧ unconditional love

✧ enough time not to be hurried

✧ freedom from major distractions

This is why it is wise to set aside special time for the two of you to "get caught up" on your love talk, on your heart talk, on your intimacy times. You can catch up each year on or around your anniversary, on vacations, or on getaway weekends.

The questions in this book are provided to help you in your intimate, emotional time together. We hope these questions can maximize those few times where you are free to open up your heart and be as spiritually, physically, socially, maritally, and financially naked as possible for a few unguarded hours of conversation.

To help you get to know your life mate at an even deeper level, we have created more than 200 "wide open communication" questions that can clarify, deepen, and strengthen your relationship. These questions cover most of the major areas you face as a couple.

In creating these questions, we have remembered our counseling sessions with young couples soon to be married, happily married couples, and unhappily married couples. We have recalled discussions in our own marriage. We remembered happy times, sad times, explosive times, loving times, and resolution times. Then we created questions we ask ourselves whenever we find ourselves with some extended time away.

The more you know about how your lifemate thinks and feels about a wide variety of issues, and the more discussions you have *in the relaxed times of your marriage*, the fewer hard times you encounter later.

A few days away is a unique period of both intimate love and intimate candor. It is a time of opening one's heart at a level never before experienced. It is a time of sharing dreams, hopes, fears, and concerns at a much more candid level than possible early in a marriage. You will have time to talk for hours, instead of only the few minutes a busy schedule will allow when you return. Take full advantage of this time to work out any concerns in your relationship—while you have hours on the beach, while you have time away from life's day-to-day pressures.

Chapter 2

The Red / Yellow / Green System—
Finding "Land Mines" before They Explode

The questions in this book uncover assumptions which might otherwise become invisible "landmines" which explode unexpectedly and cause major damage under daily pressures. These questions provide a "shovel" you can use to dig out the emotional mines before you step on them at just the wrong time back home.

We do not want to put unnecessary stress on a relationship, but rather simply bring to light those areas in which there is existing agreement or disagreement. This then gives you opportunity to fully enjoy your agreements and to fully explore your disagreements.

As you discuss the questions in this book, you may find only three or four that are potentially relationship-threatening disagreements. Work through these potentially explosive areas during your emotional intimacy catch-up time, away from pressures and day-to-day stresses.

Suppose you put off the critical discussions on these issues until you are in the midst of the daily grind of sick children and heavy financial pressures. If some problem arises and one of these major areas of disagreement must be faced under pressure, it creates a serious situation in your marriage.

Red / Yellow / Green

A great way to communicate your agreement, or lack of agreement, on each question is the "red/yellow/green light" technique. After you have thoroughly discussed a question, simply mark the question with a pencil in the margin using an *R* (red, for total disagreement), *Y* (yellow, for different conclusions or misunderstanding), or *G* (green, for total agreement).

When you finish the book, expect to have many greens in each of the seven sections, a few yellows, and hopefully very few reds. Once a question is green, you might even want to use a bright green marking pen or pencil to highlight those questions so you can see at a glance just how much you already agree. It's satisfying and reassuring!

Some of the questions do not require that you agree on an "answer"; you are just sharing personal experiences with each other. In that case, just mark it green when you have finished your discussion.

Go back to the yellow questions and discuss them until they turn green or red. Of the questions you mark red, there may be only two or three that actually represent "divorce potential" kinds of conflict. See chapter 11, "How to Turn a Red Light to Green," for help in processing these questions.

Talk It Out / Write It Out

One of the advantages of these questions is that you can simply talk them out, especially on long getaway weekends.

Although it might sound like a lot of work at first, writing out your thoughts and feelings actually has many advantages:

- ✧ Writing gives you time to reflect on the question and think more about your answers.

- ✧ You have a chance to present your answer in totality, without the risk of being interrupted.

- ✧ Some people find it easier to write something very personal than actually say it out loud.

Whichever way you discuss these questions, we hope you thoroughly enjoy the process, and that the experience helps you and your lifemate communicate your thoughts, feelings, dreams, and concerns clearly.

Chapter 3

Getting Started

There are different ways you can approach this book. Here are a few ideas:

◇ Start with the first category (financial) and proceed down the questions one by one until you have answered them all. Then go to the next category and do the same. Don't forget to mark each question red, yellow, or green.

◇ Decide together on one of the seven areas that particularly interests you at the moment (you do not have to start with financial). Start with the first question and work your way down, marking each one red, yellow, or green. There is plenty of space so you can make notes in the book about your thoughts.

◇ Answer three questions (or however many you decide) in one category. When those questions have been marked red, yellow, or green, then go to the next chapter and do three questions from that category. After you have answered three from each category, go back and answer three more from each category, and so on.

However you do it, we strongly suggest in each category that you follow the questions in order. By doing so, you eliminate the frustration of trying to find the "perfect" next question.

If you come to a question that does not apply to your relationship, just skip it and move on. Or, if a question seems too sensitive to discuss, mark it red and come back to it later.

As you answer each of the questions, you will undoubtedly think of additional questions. Write them down in the margin before you forget them.

✧

PART TWO

Anniversary / Getaway Questions

The questions in this book are divided among seven basic areas of life:

Financial
Marriage and Family
Personal Growth
Physical
Professional
Social
Spiritual

These seven categories have been listed alphabetically, but this is not to imply that the first on the list (financial) is more important than the last (spiritual). Note that God is not limited to the spiritual category. God is the God of families, commerce, hearts, minds, bodies, businesses, and societies, as well as the Lord of His church. So feel free to bring up the spiritual element in the discussion of any of the other categories.

If you have read any of the other books in the *Heart to Heart Series*, you may notice that some of the questions are repeated. You may have answered the same questions six months or a year ago, but now you are in an entirely new situation. You've grown; your mate has grown. You may give a very different answer or see the question from an entirely new perspective.

Chapter 4

Financial

There are few areas of married life which cause more yelling, pouting, and throwing of things than the financial area.

To the extent that you are making different financial assumptions, it is likely that you will go through your marriage with some severe strains in this area. Discussing your financial assumptions will help reduce the amount of frustration, pressure, and tension you experience in this area.

Make doubly sure your assumptions are compatible in this area today, and you will be half as likely to divorce because of financial tensions tomorrow!

1. How do you feel about us both working outside the home this next year?

2. How much income would you like us to make (together) this next year?

3. In today's economy, how expensive a house (in your dreams) do you want to live in? In five years? Ten years? Twenty years?

4. What do you think about credit cards? Which cards should we keep (if any)?

5. What are your feelings about a/our monthly budget?

6. What do we need to do about my car, your car, our car? What kind of car would you ideally like to drive? In five years? Ten years? Twenty years?

7. About how much do we need to spend on clothing during this year? How much would you like to spend a year in five years? In ten years?

8. Are you comfortable the way we are handling the checks to pay our monthly household bills? The bank statement each month? Our checking accounts?

9. How much money should we spend on furniture next year? Why? What are your feelings about buying good used furniture? What furniture style do you really prefer?

10. Do we need to update our will?

11. How much money should we be spending a year on luxury items such as jewelry, furs, athletic equipment, trips, etc.?

12. Are you comfortable with the amount I tip a server who does an outstanding job? Average job? Poor job?

13. Today, if we inherited a million dollars, what would you want to do with it?

14. What percent of our income should we give to the church we attend? Why?

15. What percent of our income should we give to non-profit organizations? Which ones?

16. How much life insurance should we have? Do we have adequate health insurance?

17. How do you feel about the money we invest? When should we invest more? Are you comfortable with the person who does our investing? Why?

18. How do you feel about borrowing money from our parents or relatives?

19. How do you feel about loaning money to our parents or relatives?

20. How much should we spend on a getaway weekend at this point in our lives?

21. How would you have the most amount of fun if we only had five dollars to spend some evening?

22. At our current financial level, how much should we spend on special occasions like:

    ❖ Birthdays: each other's; parents; children; friends; others (you name)

    ❖ Anniversaries: ours; parents; friends; relatives; others

    ❖ Other special days: Mother's Day; Father's Day; Valentine's Day

    ❖ Christmas: each other's gift; parents; children; other relatives; coworkers; friends; Christmas tree; decorations?

23. What should be the dollar limit on purchases made without the other's knowledge? Why?

Chapter 5

Marriage and Family

As you know by now, the lifemate decision you made is not just the one person to whom you promised to love for a lifetime. A number of other things have been determined by your marriage:

❖ your mother-in-law

❖ your father-in-law

❖ your children's grandparents

❖ your nieces and nephews, and all of the rest of your in-laws

❖ where you, and your children, will likely spend Thanksgiving, Christmas, and birthdays for the next fifty-plus years.

The success or failure of your marriage impacts a lot of people. Communicate honestly and clearly on these issues. Your extended family for generations to come will be influenced by your discussions and your decisions.

1. How often do you feel it is important to go out to dinner rather than cook at home?

2. Ideally, how would you like to celebrate our wedding anniversary each year (in general)?

3. Is there something fun or special you've always wanted us to do, but we haven't yet had the money or taken the time?

4. What do you picture us doing on our next vacation?

5. Ideally, how many children would you want to have? When? Why?

6. How do you think you would respond if we had a severely disabled child?

7. What three things do you expect to be most rewarding about parenting? What are the three most frustrating things?

8. What are the five things you definitely want me to do for and with our children?

9. What do you see as your role as a parent with our children? My role?

10. What do you want to be the five most strictly enforced rules of our house?

11. What five to ten foundational biblical truths do you think should be stressed with the children?

12. What are your thoughts and feelings about abortion?

13. What would you do if one of our children wanted to marry someone of another race or ethnic group?

14. How often should we have a getaway weekend away from the kids, leaving them with baby-sitters?

15. How do you honestly feel about nursery schools? About day-care centers? What are the advantages? Disadvantages?

16. How should we change our style of discipline with a toddler? Elementary-age child? Junior higher? High schooler? College-age?

17. What do you think about having our elementary-age children in Sunday School or church? Junior highers? High schoolers?

18. Do you think elementary-age children should be in a public or private school? What about home schooling? What about older children? Why?

19. At what age should a son begin to date? When should a daughter begin to date? What should be our house rules for curfew?

20. How much of our children's college education should we pay? Under what conditions?

21. How much freedom and responsibility should children be given at age five? Ten? Fifteen?

22. How do you feel about male or female surgery to avoid having more children? At what number of children, or under what circumstances, would you consider it necessary to take precautions not to have more children? ·

23. Are there areas in which we may be a bad example to our children? What can we do about this?

24. What does the phrase "Till death do us part" actually mean to you?

25. Do you see divorce as an option in any circumstances? If so, in what circumstances?

26. If there has been divorce in your immediate family, what preventive steps can we take today to avoid similar disruptive patterns in our relationship?

27. When we disagree with one another, how can we be more effective in resolving our differences?

28. What do you think about marital counseling? Do you feel it would be helpful for us to have some counseling right now? Why? What are the advantages? Done by whom?

29. What are the five things you like best about our married life together?

30. What are your five greatest concerns or lingering questions about our marriage?

31. How do you feel about the amount of television our family watches? The type of programs? Do we need to make any adjustments in this area?

32. How can we keep the romance alive in our marriage? (Be specific.) How important to you are those elements in our marriage?

33. What kind of music do you really like? Really dislike?

34. What are three of your happiest memories of our life together so far? Why?

35. What is your favorite thing to do that we don't do very much anymore?

36. What couple, whom you know personally, has the most ideal marriage? Why do you think it is so ideal?

37. Deep down, how does your mother feel about our relationship? Your father? Brothers and sisters?

38. What are the three things you admire most about each of your parents as a marriage partner?

39. What are the three things you admire most about your parents as people?

40. If one of our parents became widowed or seriously ill, what would you think should be our responsibility to him/her?

41. Do you feel that any of our relatives are interfering in our marriage? Who? How? What should we do about it?

42. What pet peeves do I seem insensitive to at this point in our relationship?

43. Are you happy with who does what in our family at this point? What do you think should be changed? Why?

44. What are your three favorite thoughts about our making love?

45. What are five things you like best about how I make love?

46. What are the things that are uncomfortable to you, or you would rather not do anymore, in our lovemaking?

47. From your perspective, what are the most important things to be aware of when we are making love?

48. What surprised you most the first time we made love?

49. What have you wanted to say about our lovemaking for some time but have been waiting for just the right time to bring it up? Why is this so important to you?

Chapter 6

Personal Growth

Remember back ten years. Talk about what life was like for each of you then. Could you possibly have imagined where you would be today?

It would have been just as easy for you to imagine today ten years ago as it would be to imagine ten years from now—today!

Point: You will both continue to grow rapidly, but how do you each want to grow, and in what direction? Where do you each feel held back?

1. A year from today, in what three to five areas of your life would you most like to be stronger than you are now?

2. In what three areas would you most like to see me grow in the next year? Why?

3. What do you feel are the three key things keeping you from reaching your full potential as a person today?

4. If you could become the "world expert" in any one area or subject, what would it be?

5. In what area would you suggest I specialize and become expert?

6. What five books would you most like to read?

7. If you could sit and chat with any person in the world, with whom would you talk? What three questions would you ask that person?

8. What do you consider your three greatest strengths to be maximized in the future? What is your single greatest strength?

9. If we could improve only one aspect of the way we relate to each other, what would that be? Why?

10. What keeps you from getting excited about being promoted at work or taking on more responsibility?

11. What negative comment did someone make about you years ago which is still holding back your confidence? How can I help you overcome that blockage in your life?

12. In what three areas of your life do you think you have grown most in the last several years?

13. What three people have had the greatest impact in your life? How?

14. Who was your best friend in grade school? Junior high? High school? College? How did each contribute to your personal growth at that time of your life?

15. If you had four hours in which to do anything you wanted, what would you do? Why? If you had a weekend?

Chapter 7

Physical

One basic reality in life is: We all change physically as we grow older. What are your thoughts about your own physical appearance and that of your life partner?

How do you actually *feel* about your weight, your sex appeal, and your overall image?

1. How do you feel about an exercise program for you and me? What kind? How often?

2. What kind of physical exercise would you most like to do together? Separately?

3. What five things do you like best about my physical appearance, in general?

4. What three suggestions would you like to make about how I can improve my physical appearance? My overall image?

5. How do you feel about taking vitamins and nutritional supplements? How much per month should be spent on them?

6. Would you prefer to go to a medical doctor or a nutritionist?

7. How do you feel about going to chiropractors?

8. How do you feel about the food we eat? What changes would you make? Are you willing to help make changes (shopping, cooking, studying, etc.)?

9. Based on your family's medical history, do you have any anxieties about your health either now or in the future? How would you feel if I developed one of these conditions?

10. How do you feel about me being overweight? How do you feel about you being overweight? How many pounds do you think is overweight?

11. How do you feel about baldness? Wrinkles? Gray hair?

12. Do you have a desire to belong to a health club? Why?

13. What do you consider your very favorite recreational activity?

14. How do you honestly feel about getting older? Thirty? Forty? Fifty? Sixty? Seventy?

15. Specifically, what should we do to avoid the potential of having an affair?

16. How do you prefer I wear my hair? How do you feel about beards, mustaches, sideburns? How many buttons should I leave open on a shirt or blouse?

17. What kind of pajamas do you find the most exciting, pleasing, ideal?

18. What is your favorite outfit/clothing, and why do you enjoy it?

19. What five nationally known personalities do you most identify with and would ideally like to be like in some way? Why?

20. Who are five people you find most attractive sexually, and what is it about them that you find attractive? How will you deal with the difference between what you find attractive in others of the opposite sex and what I am not?

21. What "turns you off" sexually? What "turns you on" sexually?

22. Does the difference in our natural energy level bother you in any way?

Chapter 8

Professional

As a person matures he/she moves through phases like:

"I got the job!"

"I think I'll choose this field as my profession."

"My career is progressing well . . . or is in a slump."

"What should my lifework be?"

As each of you progresses in age and professional experience, it is critical that you are both making the same basic assumptions concerning your professions!

1. How do you feel about my work? What do you like best about it? Is there anything about my work that frustrates or worries you? Are you proud of the work I do?

2. What type of work do you think I would do best?

3. What would you consider my top three alternative careers? Why do you think these would be good things for me to pursue?

4. To what professional or work-related associations or groups should you, or I, or we belong? Why?

5. What company, organization, or firm would you most like to work with if you had your choice? Why?

6. How would you feel about my working with the _____ company?

7. What do you consider the five most important factors in bringing you happiness or satisfaction in your work? How many of those factors are present in your work now?

8. What work-related or professional goals will you have to reach to feel really successful in life?

9. What kind of work brings you the most personal fulfillment?

10. How important to you is the feeling that you are making a significant difference in your work?

11. How important is it to you to have fun on your job?

12. How important to you is being a member of the team at work? Of being accepted by that team?

13. What will you have to learn, do, or become before you are ready for the next promotion at work?

14. How important is *security* in any career you would choose? Why?

15. How do you feel about a job or career for me that would include travel? How much travel would be acceptable to you? How much would you consider to be unacceptable?

16. How important to you is our parents' acceptance of what we do as a profession?

17. Would you rather work with your hands, your head, or your back?

18. If you could have anyone's job in the world, whose job would you have and why?

19. What do you definitely and absolutely *not* want in your lifework?

20. How would you feel about us working together as a two-person team at some time in the future? If you would feel good about that, what would you see us doing together?

21. How do you feel about a wife having a separate career from her husband, where she may need as much support to keep going in her profession as the husband would in his?

22. How would you feel about me making more (or less) money than you, if that should happen?

23. What is it in a job or career that you would definitely *not* want me to be part of in the future?

24. If my work responsibilities required me to move to another location, in what parts of the country/world would you feel comfortable living? Where would you definitely *not* want to live? Why?

25. Under what circumstances do you feel a wife should (should not) work outside the home?

26. How would you feel about me working two jobs?

27. How do you think your father feels (felt) about his work? How do you feel about his work?

28. When you were growing up, did your mother work outside the home? Either way, how did you feel about it? Why?

29. What is the highest position you can imagine me holding at some time in the future?

30. How would you feel about me if next year I became a full-time Christian minister? Corporate executive? Factory worker? Farmer? Lawyer? Medical professional (doctor, nurse, etc.)? Missionary? Movie star? Psychologist? Police officer? Politician? Rock singer? Salesperson? Self-employed? Truck driver?

31. How would you feel about starting a business from scratch where there was a major risk to the money we invested from our savings?

32. Would you prefer that I be on a lower fixed salary or a higher potential commission with no guaranteed income? Why?

33. If I decided to go back to school for further education, how would you feel about that decision? What would be the advantages? Disadvantages?

34. If you could start a business with anyone, what three people would you choose to be partners? Why?

35. If we started a business together, what would you want to do in that business?

36. Would you hesitate to start a business of our own? Why?

Chapter 9

Social

$\mathbb{F}$riendships are invaluable! Social times are priceless! However, are we making the same assumptions about our social life? Do we really enjoy the same people, the same parties, or entertaining in the same way?

1. How have our social relationships with each of our single friends changed now that we are married? Are there any you would like to rekindle?

2. One year from now, what difference would you hope there would be in our social life? In five years?

3. How do you feel about me going "out with the guys" (or gals, friends of the same gender)? How often do you feel comfortable with me being out with friends?

4. How do you feel about parties? What kind do you most enjoy? Least enjoy? Want to avoid at all costs?

5. What's the best party you have ever attended? Why did you enjoy it so much?

6. How confident are you socially, on a scale of one to ten (where one is insecure and ten is extremely confident)? How does your confidence at a party change

when we are there together, as compared to your being there alone?

7. Who do you consider to be your five closest friends? Why do you enjoy them? Are you uncomfortable with any of my best friends? Why?

8. When going out for a social evening, what do you enjoy doing most with another couple or small group of people?

9. How do you feel about having friends "pop in"? Your relatives? My relatives?

10. How do you feel about us "popping in" on friends? Your relatives? My relatives?

11. How do you feel about having out-of-town friends stay overnight with us? Out-of-town relatives?

12. How do you feel about staying with friends when we travel (as opposed to staying in hotels)?

13. If we were to take an automobile/van trip with another couple within five hundred miles of home, what would you want to do? How long would you want to stay? Where would you want to go? With whom?

14. How many nights a month would you be open to guests staying in our home?

15. What qualities do you think my friends have in common? What do you think I look for in a friend?

16. What do you think I give to a friendship?

17. What puts pressure on you socially? Why?

18. How do you feel about your parents' social life? How do you feel about my parents' social life?

19. How would you improve on our social lives?

20. Who do you consider your top three lifelong friends—friends you'd like to remain close to twenty, forty years from today? Why in each case? How do you feel about each of my three closest friends?

21. What are the social situations in which you feel least comfortable and why?

22. What are the social situations in which you feel most confident? Why?

23. What do you most enjoy doing on an evening out? Why?

24. What are the elements of a social event that make you frustrated? Disappointed? Angry? Uncomfortable?

25. If you could go to any "high society" event in the world, what event would you most enjoy attending?

26. If you could go back in history, what social event would you most enjoy attending? Why?

27. If we were given $2,000 to go somewhere just for fun, where would you want to go? Why?

28. If we had $200 to spend socially, how would you want to spend it?

29. If we had only $20 to do something "wild and crazy" together socially, what would you want to do? Why?

30. What kind of parties do you find most enjoyable (theme parties, costume parties, Valentine parties, Christmas parties, etc.)?

31. If we were to go to dinner on three separate evenings with three different couples, what three couples would you most enjoy going to dinner with? Why in each case?

32. If we were to go with one couple to some foreign country, what country would you want to visit? With whom?

33. How many evenings a week (or a month) would you enjoy socializing with friends? Why?

34. On a Friday or Saturday night, if the choice was between staying home and reading, or going out to a movie or party, which would you honestly prefer?

Chapter 10

Spiritual

Two American taboos of polite conversation are politics and religion. In marriage, however, these topics are "must discussions"!

Take your time and discuss each of these questions as openly as humanly possible.

1. When you lean back in your chair and imagine heaven, what do you see?

2. How do you feel about our church?

3. Is our church teaching the truths of the Bible?

4. What do you enjoy doing or being involved with in a church?

5. What type of worship service do you prefer?

6. Ideally, how often would you like us to read the Bible together? Why?

7. How would you describe your prayer life?

8. How do you feel about our having a devotional time together?

9. How would you feel about my being a member of the clergy someday? Why?

10. What are the three highlights of your spiritual life so far?

11. What has been the low point of your spiritual life?

12. What are some important, nonnegotiable, biblical issues, principles, or doctrines? Why?

13. If you could ask God any three questions on any topic, what would you ask? Why?

14. What do you believe the Bible says about marriage and divorce?

15. How do you feel about and think about Jesus?

16. In what area of your spiritual life do you feel the greatest need for personal growth? Is there any way I can help you in these areas?

17. If I felt "led of God" to move to Africa and work with some tribal group, what would be your reaction?

18. What do you believe about hell? About heaven?

19. How confident are you right now of your salvation?

20. Is there a specific church or denomination that is important to you? Why? Is there a particular church or denomination you would *not* want to be involved with? Why?

21. What do you believe is God's standard regarding sexual relationships within marriage? Do you believe there are any biblical limits to our sexual relationship?

22. From a biblical perspective, what do you believe to be the husband's responsibility to his wife? To his children? To the spiritual welfare of his wife and

children? What are examples of practical ways you see this responsibility being carried out in our marriage?

23. From a biblical perspective, what do you believe to be the wife's responsibility to her husband? To her children? To the spiritual welfare of her husband and children? What are examples of practical ways you see this responsibility being carried out in our marriage?

24. How do you feel about tithing (giving 10 percent) regularly to your church?

PART THREE

Taking Action

*This book is intended to maximize
your marriage.*

Although some of the questions may seem
threatening, look at them as an
opportunity to learn more about yourself
as well as your partner.

Chapter 11

_____

*How to Turn
a Red Light to Green*

If you and your spouse disagree on a question, the first thing you ask is: "Is this an important issue to me? To us?" If your difference of opinion is on something that *both* of you consider insignificant, then you don't need to read any further.

However, if the red light is an issue of significance to *either one* of you, there are several conflict-resolution skills or approaches available. We will not list them *all* for you. Our objective is to give you a few ideas on how to approach the conflict. They may or may not work for every yellow or red issue, but you should be able to make headway toward a green.

If these ideas do not work, we suggest that together you seek a wise friend or a qualified minister or counselor. Tell that person what you have discussed so far about the issue. Never be concerned or embarrassed in seeking help. A marriage is a precious asset and should be nurtured and cared for with wisdom. Marriage often takes more wisdom than any two people alone can provide.

Unfortunately, many times, either the husband or wife won't even consider talking to a counselor until one announces he or she is leaving the relationship. Then the reluctant one is willing to talk, but in many cases it is too little, too late.

Ideas to Consider

1. Express your thoughts and feelings openly yet sensitively. You cannot resolve a difference if you choose to be passive or silent.

2. Commit to the resolution of the disagreement and work on it. You cannot resolve a difference if one partner chooses to be less than 100 percent involved in making it work.

3. Realize the importance of the resolution of serious conflict. You can certainly live together without red lights resolved, but your relationship will be weakened and possibly vulnerable to problems.

It is our prayer that these questions helped you see with crystal clarity that your mate is your lifelong friend and spouse. We feel honored that you let us be a part of your growth together.

Chapter 12

Ten Ways to Keep Your Marriage Healthy and Happy

The following ten suggestions will help keep you focused on developing a healthy, happy marriage.

1. Commit "till death do us part"—you have made a vow to God and to another much-loved human being.
   - Dream together—look forward to things.
   - Be loyal to your mate at all costs.
   - Care more about what your mate thinks of you than what your friends do.

2. Develop a common spiritual commitment.
   - Pray for your mate regularly.
   - Pray together regularly.
   - Worship together.

3. Want what is best for your lifemate.
   - Focus on what's right with your mate, not what's wrong with him/her.
   - Work as a team—rely on each other's strength.

❖ Serve your mate.

4. Spend time with model couples who have been happily married ten to twenty years longer than you.

❖ Develop a relationship with a personal mentor to help you when times are tough, giving you wise counsel.

❖ Spend time with peer couples that have healthy, happy marriages.

5. Understand that no marriage and no partner is perfect. Give grace to be different.

❖ No one wants to fail. Your mate is doing the best he/she can at the moment.

❖ Don't take all emotional explosions personally. Sometimes your mate just needs to let off steam!

❖ Let the relationship breathe. A couple needs time together and away. When things get tense, you may just need a few hours or days away.

6. Find time to communicate—walking on the beach, telephoning, traveling together.

❖ Communicating your heart
—Listen to your mate's heart, not just to words.
—Let your mate vent emotions without feeling you have to "fix it"!

❖ Settling differences
—Don't pout; stay and talk it out.
—"Clarify" concerns if you don't like to "confront."
—Listen carefully. Allow your mate to complete his or her thoughts without you interrupting, moving off the subject, or waiting impatiently to make your point.

7. Develop common interests.
   - Enjoy hobbies and friends.
   - Do fun things together—concerts, plays, picnics.
   - Travel together whenever you get a chance.

8. Get to know your mate at the deepest level possible.
   - Study your mate—what turns her/him off and on sexually, nonverbal signals, foreplay, moods, etc.
   - Know precisely what your mate needs from you.

9. Avoid:
   - negative kidding—saying negative things you don't really mean that secretly hurt and do serious damage to one's confidence and one's natural love;
   - conditional love—basing love on actions of any kind;
   - waiting for your mate to meet your needs before you will meet hers/his;
   - talking negatively about your mate's parents.

10. Be romantic, not just sexy.
    - Splurge occasionally.
    - Do small things which communicate "Thinking only of you . . . Thought of you while I was away . . . You are the center of my universe!"
    - Start foreplay ten minutes after climax, not ten minutes before climax.
    - Talk with a loving, caring, tender tone in your voice, not an angry, harsh, bitter tone.

✧

Ten Affordable Ways to Rekindle Your Romance

1. Take a little time off work—walk on the beach or in a forest, prepare a picnic away from everyone and everything, alone together.

2. Say "I love you" ten ways in one day without words.

3. Share something from your heart with your mate you have never told anyone about yourself.

4. Express every positive thought/feeling you have: "You smell good, I like your hairstyle, you have great hands, your voice is like the wind" (whatever you do, do not add "like a tornado"!).

5. Make your bedroom a special romantic place: use candles, lights, lace, etc.

6. Attend weddings and funerals together. It reminds you how fortunate you are to be alive and in love!

7. Give a few flowers, a bit of poetry, or a simple "just thinking of you" gift.

8. Call in the middle of the day just to say "I love you!"

9. A simple greeting card for no reason is very romantic—especially if it contains a short, loving, handwritten expression of the true love in your heart.

10. A full body massage is always nice—and is always affordable.

We hope these ten suggestions are as helpful to you as they have been to us.

Conclusion

It is interesting to take notice of the questions you found to be uncomfortable—these are indicators of areas where it would be helpful to grow in your relationship together. As you both have a better understanding of each other, you will be able to handle the stresses that inevitably come in a marriage.

Disagreements on basic issues—unresolved red lights—need not be marriage breakers. You may just need help sorting out assumptions, understanding motivations, and clearing up communication. Don't hesitate to seek the help of a counselor to work through these differences. After all, a lifetime vow is at stake.

These questions are not for one-time use. You can discuss your way through them each time you get away for the rest of your life and have fresh answers and gain new insights each time.

Your marriage should be based on a relationship which is secure, lasting, and mutually beneficial. It's our prayer that these questions have helped you along that journey!

Appendix

*Additional Resources
by Bobb and Cheryl Biehl*

Asking to Win!

This booklet (part of our Pocket Confidence series) goes in your suit coat pocket, briefcase, or purse. It contains one hundred questions—ten questions to ask in each of the following situations:

1. Asking—personal questions to avoid "small talk"

2. Brainstorming—to maximize your very finest ideas

3. Career-ing—when you or a friend are considering changing careers

4. Deciding—when a risky, pressurized, costly decision needs to be made

5. Interviewing—getting behind the smile of a potential team member

6. Focusing—putting your life into focus, or refocus

7. Organizing—to maximize your time

8. Parenting—to raise healthy, balanced children.

9. Planning—any organization or major project

10. Solving—questions to solve problems faster

These booklets are packaged/priced reasonably enough for you to give to adult children, colleagues, friends, proteges, spouses, staff members.

Career Change Questions / Lifework

Thirty Questions to Ask before Making Any Major Career Change.

This series of thirty questions comes in handy any time you are thinking about the possibility of making a career change. These questions save you hours of uncertainty.

Time-Focusing Questions

If it seems you just never have time as a couple to do what you most want to do, consider listening to this tape together and making some specific prioritizing decisions.

Executive Evaluation-135

Have you ever wanted a comprehensive evaluation checklist for telling your mate exactly how he or she is doing, on a 1–10 scale, in everything from bad breath to decision making? This is it—135 dimensions in all. This is an ideal annual tool for you to use with those close to you. And, if you like, let them evaluate you. This list helps maximize communication while concentrating on the positive.

Focusing Your Life

"Focusing Your Life" is a simple, step-by-step process you learn in about three hours. It helps "clear the fog" and keeps you focused for the rest of your life. This great, personal retreat guide helps you reflect on your future!

Mentoring: How to Find One and How to Become One

This booklet gives you very useful steps about forming a mentoring relationship and answers practical mentoring questions with tried and true answers. Consider finding a mentor couple to help you through some of the tight places in life.

Mentoring Wisdom

As a couple you can grow together in your ability to provide wise leadership for your family and in work settings. These principles are fun to read and discuss on a long vacation drive or when conversation gets a little stale and you need a small spark to get your discussion started. There are approximately two hundred quotable leadership principles, rules of thumb, and observations which are key to generating creative ideas and gaining objective perspective!

On My Own Handbook

If you have been increasingly concerned about your high school or college student's readiness to face the "real world," this book has been written for your son or daughter. Many adults have said that they wish their parents had taught them these principles before they started off "on their own." Parents, as well as students, benefit from these extremely fundamental leadership principles. These principles will stay with your son or daughter for a lifetime. And they likely will pass many on to their children's children.

Heart to Heart Series

We want you to have a perfect marriage, or as close to it as possible. These four affordable paperback books help you ask fresh, stimulating, fun, intimate, enlightening questions of your mate, to make sure your marriage has as solid a foundation as possible.

Premarriage Questions—Fun questions to ask before you get married, to help you have a healthy, happy, lifelong marriage.

Newly Married Questions—Intimate questions to ask each other on your honeymoon, to make sure you are bonded emotionally as well as physically as you start your life together.

Anniversary Questions—Stimulating questions to ask yourself on any anniversary, marriage retreat, or getaway weekend, to make sure your lines of communication are wide open!

Pre-remarriage Questions—Questions to ask before you remarry, to protect you both at this vulnerable time.

Stop Setting Goals

When a husband is a goal setter and the wife a problem solver, there are many predictable problems. When a wife is a goal setter and the husband is a problem solver, there are many predictable problems. When both husband and wife are goal setters or both problem solvers, there are many predictable problems. This book helps you determine which you are, and how (as a couple) to maximize your differences instead of being hurt by them.

The Question Book

A high percentage of marital frustration, tension, and pressure comes in the decision-making process. But when unwise decisions are made without asking the basic, probing questions, it adds to the household tension.

Ninety-nine experts give you the twenty questions they would teach their own son or daughter to ask before making an important decision in their area of expertise.

The Question Book is a lifelong reference book. Written in a classic style, it will never really be "out of date." Topics are alphabetically easy to find.

Where to Focus When Your Life's a Blur

Do you find yourself juggling the many hats of household taxi, travel agent, correspondent, nurse, tutor, coach, encyclopedia, psychologist, nutritionist, referee, and answering machine? If this sounds familiar, this book gives practical, step-by-step help in sorting out your priorities and making choices that are best for you.

Why You Do What You Do

This book is a result of more than 21,000 hours of behind-the-lines experiences with some of the finest, emotionally healthy leaders of our generation. This model was developed to maximize "healthy" people with a few emotional "mysteries" still unanswered! It answers questions (about your spouse) like:

- ✧ Why does he/she have a phobic fear of failure, rejection, or insignificance?
- ✧ Why is he/she so "driven" to be admired, recognized, appreciated, secure, respected, or accepted?
- ✧ Why is he/she an enabler, leader, promoter, rescuer, controller, people-pleaser?
- ✧ Why is he/she a perfectionist, workaholic, or "withdrawer" from tough situations?
- ✧ Where is he/she most vulnerable to the temptation of an affair?
- ✧ Why does he/she have such a hard time relating to his/her parents?
- ✧ Why does he/she sometimes seem like a child?

These and other emotional mysteries can be understood and resolved in the silence of your own heart and marriage without years of therapy.

Wisdom for Men

This is a small, easy-to-read gift book for any Christian husband. It contains life principles combined with parallel Scriptures to give wise perspective on many topics.

To learn when Bobb or Cheryl will be speaking in your area, or to learn more about any of the resources listed above, contact is possible in the following ways:

WRITE:
Bobb and Cheryl Biehl
c/o Masterplanning Group International
Post Office Box 952499
Lake Mary, Florida 32795-2499

TELEPHONE:
To contact the Biehl's office (answered "Masterplanning Group"), call 1-407-330-2028

To request a complete catalogue (FREE), call 1-800-969-1976

To order materials, call 1-800-443-1976.

FAX:
1-407-333-4134